INCREDIBLY COLORFUL CREATURES

by Megan Cooley Peterson

CAPSTONE PRESS
a capstone imprint

Published by Spark, an imprint of Capstone.
1710 Roe Crest Drive, North Mankato, Minnesota 56003
capstonepub.com

Library of Congress Cataloging-in-Publication Data is available on the Library of Congress website.
ISBN 9781666355413 (hardcover)
ISBN 9781666355420 (paperback)
ISBN 9781666355437 (ebook pdf)

Summary: Full-color photos and simple, engaging text describe a variety of extremely colorful animals, their habitats, food, and behaviors.

Image Credits
Alamy: Eng Wah Teo, 23, George Grill, 25, Jason Edwards, 13, Paul Harrison, 4; Science Source: Adam Fletcher, 29, Gary Meszaros, 19; Shutterstock: A. Kehinde, 17, ArCaLu, 5, 14, Cingular, Cover (top), Elocin Nadroj, Cover (bottom), fenkieandreas, 11, fntproject, 27, Jay Ondreicka, 18, 26, Jesus Cobaleda, 7, Joe Belanger, 9, Kletr, 10, nwdph, 15, Sara Nadeea, 6, slowmotiongli, 21

Design Elements
Shutterstock: Cassel

Editorial Credits
Editor: Erika L. Shores; Designer: Hilary Wacholz; Media Researcher: Jo Miller; Production Specialist: Tori Abraham

All internet sites appearing in back matter were available and accurate when this book was sent to press.

Printed and bound in the USA. PO4882

TABLE OF CONTENTS

Words in **bold** are in the glossary.

WARNING: BRIGHT COLORS AHEAD

Move over, brown bears. Step away, gray elephants. The flashy creatures in this book aren't afraid of a little color—or a lot! Some are so wild they almost look fake. But all the animals in this book are real.

COLORS IN THE SEA

ONE-TWO PUNCH

One of nature's best hunters packs a big punch. The peacock mantis shrimp attacks with its hammer claws. These punches move as fast as a bullet.

FACT

The peacock mantis shrimp has unusual eyeballs. They can look in two directions at the same time. Each eye moves on its own.

The mantis shrimp's colorful body blends in with the coral reef. It sneaks up on its food. Wham! Then it bashes through the animal's shell.

SUNGLASSES NEEDED

Grab some sunglasses when you look at this animal. It seems to glow. Spanish shawl sea slugs have **neon** purple bodies. On top grows an orange, fingerlike fringe.

The food these sea slugs eat gives them their amazing colors. Spanish shawls also get stinging **cells** from their food. They store them in their fringe. Zap! An animal got too close!

fringe

COLOR MAZE

How do you know Mandarin fish like mazes? Because they wear them on their bodies. Red, orange, and yellow lines swirl across these fish. The bright colors let other animals know to stay away.

COLORS IN THE TREES

HANDS OFF!

Don't eat me! The wattle cup caterpillar's dazzling colors send a warning. Its colors scare off most attackers. Sharp **spines** also get the job done. Each spine is filled with poison. Getting stung by this insect hurts!

FACT
The wattle cup caterpillar turns into a cream and brown moth. Boring. But its dull colors keep it hidden.

STEALING THE SHOW

Here's a bird that takes colorful to the next level. Its rainbow-like feathers come in eight colors. Both the male and female lilac breasted roller are brightly colored.

Rollers are super fliers. They sit high in the tops of trees. Lizards and bugs crawl on the ground below. The birds then dive for the kill.

SMELLY WORK OF ART

Can a bug be a work of art? Check out the Picasso bug. It has spots of blue, green, and red. These colors tell other animals to back off. The bug can also let out a gross smell when it's scared. Hungry animals move on to a less stinky meal.

FACT

The Picasso bug was named after Pablo Picasso. This famous artist painted with bright colors.

NOW YOU SEE ME,
NOW YOU DON'T

Is that flying cotton candy? No, it's the rosy maple moth. It's bright pink and yellow. This tricky bug can hide in plain sight. Rosy maple moths live in maple trees. Their bodies look like maple tree seed cases. Birds can't see them.

SHOWING OFF

Did those birds just play a game of paintball? Gouldian finches have red, yellow, or black heads. Males have brighter purple feathers than females. Males puff up and bob their heads. They use their beautiful feathers to find a mate.

FACT
Gouldian finches get their bright colors from the seeds they eat.

COLORS ON THE GROUND

SCALY SECRETS

This snake's electric blue and red scales hide its secret weapon. The Asian blue coral snake has some of the strongest **venom** on Earth. It uses it to feed on other deadly snakes, including cobras.

PRETTY IN POOP

Rainbow scarab beetles are hard to miss. Their bright green, red, purple, and gold bodies **shimmer**. These shiny bugs hang out someplace gross—on poop! Female scarab beetles lay their eggs in animal poop. Newly hatched **larvae** eat it. The beetle's nasty meal choice helps clean the earth.

CREEPING CRABS

Halloween crabs are dressed up and ready to trick-or-treat. They are spooky colors like red, purple, and black. And they only come out at night. The crabs creep along the forest floor. Then they drag leaves back to their homes.

EIGHT-LEGGED DANCERS

Peacock spiders are tiny. They are smaller than the eraser on a pencil. But males show off colorful designs on their fanlike tails. These jumping spiders dance to attract females. Check out those fancy tail colors as they move and groove.

FACT
Peacock spiders only live in Australia.

GLOSSARY

cell (SEL)—a basic part of an animal or plant that is so small you can't see it without a microscope

larva (LAR-vuh)—an insect at the stage of development between an egg and an adult

neon (NEE-on)—extremely bright

shimmer (SHIM-ur)—to shine or sparkle

spine (SPINE)—a long, pointed growth

venom (VEN-uhm)—a poisonous liquid produced by some animals

READ MORE

Guiraud, Florence. *Wonders of Nature: Explorations in the World of Birds, Insects, and Fish*. New York: Prestel, 2018.

Park, Jane. *Hidden Animal Colors*. Minneapolis: Millbrook Press, 2022.

Romero, Libby. *Animals That Change Color.* Washington, D.C.: National Geographic Kids, 2020.

INTERNET SITES

Animal Colors
timeforkids.com/k1/animal-colors

Animal Colors That Catch the Eye
askabiologist.asu.edu/animal-colors-and-patterns

Protective Coloration
kids.britannica.com/kids/article/protective-coloration/353670

INDEX

ABOUT THE AUTHOR

Megan Cooley Peterson has been an avid reader and writer since she was a little girl. She has written nonfiction children's books about topics ranging from urban legends to gross animal facts. She lives in Minnesota with her husband and daughter.